# VIENNA

## CITY GUIDE WITH A CITY MAP
## AND A MAP OF THE UNDERGROUND

VERLAG
**bauer**
WIEN

# INTRODUCTION

"Küss die Hand, Gnä Frau!" – Servus!" und a herzliches "Grüß Gott in Wien!" The Viennese, ever chivalrous, always full of charm, will greet a lady thus. "A kiss on the hand, honourable lady. I'm at your service – with a heartfelt greeting, by the grace of God, to Vienna." Perhaps somewhat literal in translation, but the message is clear. At the beginning of this little introduction I wish you a heartfelt welcome to Vienna, one of the most multifaceted cities in Europe. Many ethnic, cultural and political influences have given Vienna an unmistakable position in the course of history and the present day.

Seen politically, Vienna lies at the gates of the east with which the city has always enjoyed a good relationship, as a glance at the telephone book shows with its many Slavic and Hungarian names. But Vienna is also a junction between northern and southern Europe. You will hear Italian words adopted into the Viennese dialect; Bohemian and Poland have also left their traces. A focused view of these complex interrelationships will give us a brief outline of the city's history.

The Celts settle here on the trade route of the Amber Road before the birth of Christ. The Romans later construct the castle of Vindabona as a defence against the Germanic tribes, before the migration of the peoples overtakes the settlement and reduces it to insignificance for a long period. Only in 881 does the name Wenia reappear in the annals of Salzburg, thus documenting the rising importance of the region as Carolingian border marches, and later of the Ottoman Kingdom, against the Awares and Hungarian aggression from the east. The Babenbergs become margraves and later dukes of the Ostarrichi marches. They make Vienna their residence in 1155, and issue the oldest recorded city constitution in 1221. The last Babenberg falls in battle against the Hungarians in 1246 and the line dies out. Hapsburg rule begins with the vanquishing of the Bohemian King Ottokar Przemysl by the German King Rudolf I of Hapsburg. Their fate is closely associated with the rise of Vienna to a great city. Rudolf IV founds the University of Vienna in 1365.

After the Turkish march on central Europe is twice successfully hindered by Vienna, in 1529 and 1683, nothing remains to impede its growth to a great city. Baroque vitality and the wise rule of Maria Theresa (1740–1780) and her son Joseph II (1780–1790) brings the city to an incomparable period of greatness. Lukas von Hildebrandt and Johann Bernhard Fischer von Erlach form the city landscape with sumptuous churches and palaces. Haydn, Mozart, Gluck – later Beethoven and Schubert – found the high repute of Vienna as the musical capital of Europe. The invasion by Napoleon leads to a brief demise, which is followed by a renewed period of greatness. The leading heads of Europe gather at the Vienna Congress of 1814/15. Europe is reorganised, and the people indulge in euphoric festivities: "The Congress Dances." The Viennese waltz is established as an art form.

The contrasts between wealthy citizens and the crassly discriminated levels of society during the Biedermeier period becomes increasingly defined and revolution breaks out in 1848. Emperor Ferdinand I is obliged to abdicate and Franz Joseph I becomes his successor at the age of eighteen. He is to reign for 68 long years. The period brings cultural peaks such as the era of the Golden Operetta (Strauß, Suppé, Zeller, Ziehrer

rer, Millöcker); Brahms, Bruckner and Mahler create works in Vienna; the Ringstrasse is built from 1857; literature and painting blossom. But at the same time nationalism and separatism shakes the multiracial State, which finally leads to the 1914–1918 World War, which changes Europe completely. Franz Joseph does not live to see the end of the monarchy (1918), he dies in 1916 before the end of the war.

The crumbling of the old order in the course of time, and the nostalgic look to the past, releases an unbelievable cultural force; the Vienna School of Medicine around Rokitansky and Billroth revolutionise the health service of the 19th century; Sigmund Freud develops psychoanalysis; poets and writers such as Bahr, Kraus, Schnitzler, Hofmannsthal and Zweig reappraise the heritage of the monarchy; the coffee house becomes a place of literature, and Art Nouveau changes Vienna. Otto Wagner gives significant accents to city planning (city railway). Klimt is the soul of the "Secession" and with his pupils, Schiele and Kokoschka, lays the cornerstone of the modern age in Austria. The "Second Vienna School" around Schönberg, Berg and Webern, tread new paths in music.

Today, decades after the destruction of the Second World War, Vienna is changed in many ways. Once the metropolis of a great nation, Vienna is now only the capital of the small, neutral Austria. The importance of the city for an East-West dialogue, and its status in international relationships, however, has remained: Vienna has been third seat of office of the UNO since 1979.

Much of Vienna is known throughout the world: Schönbrunn, the Belvedere, the museums, the Vienna Philharmonic, the Vienna Boys' Choir, the Opera Ball and the New Years' Concert, the Festival Weeks and the Spanish Riding School, the Sachertorte and the pastries. Yet one can hardly speak of "typical Viennese" in these terms, they present only the facade, behind such contrasting vital traditions, informal intimacy and modern hectic, a will to innovation and roots in the past, defy all clichés. Describing a typical Viennese is as equally difficult. It is generally said that they are tolerant and charming. The attempt at description was made in the saga of the "Lieben Augustin", the jolly chap who, despite the pest and mass dying, still remained above it all, "armed" with a glass of wine against fate, and even against death. Qualtinger and Merz are more critical in their creation for the theatre of "Herrn Karl", the ingratiating survival artist with his pessimistic whining brutality. As different as they have always seen themselves, one thing is common to all Viennese: they swear and complain about God and creation, they grouch and prefer to be cranky and original than to be run-of-the-mill people. But don't confuse that grouching with disgust. Quite the opposite. The Viennese allow themselves to criticise only that which they love.

This little book, dear guest, will, and can only, offer an overview of the essential, but not the real Vienna, and should be taken as an invitation to linger, when it so pleases, and to go deeper into the history, tradition and present times of a delightful city.

*Wiener Neustadt Altar*

*The Virgin of Mercy*

## SAINT STEPHEN'S CATHEDRAL

On the site of this monumental building once stood a Romanesque basilica founded by Duke Heinrich II Jasomirgott in the 12th century. After the fire in 1258, the church was rebuilt in the Romanesque style. Of this building remain the round-arched giant portal with, on each side of it, the later somewhat Gothicised heathen towers. The foundation stone for the Gothic St Stephen's Cathedral was laid on April 7, 1359, by Duke Rudolf IV, giving him the name in this connection of "the founder." The south tower was completed in 1433 by Hans von Prachatitz, and the nave in 1455 by Hans Puchspaum. The building of the north tower was discontinued in 1511, presumably due to the Reformation and immediate danger of the Turks. In the last days of the Second World War the masterly woodwork of the Gothic roof frame was destroyed, but could be renewed with great effort. The landmark of the city of Vienna, the 137-metre-high St Stephen's steeple – known lovingly by the Viennese as "der Steffl" – is considered one of the most prominent examples of Gothic architecture. The watchmen's chamber, at 72 metres, served the fire brigade in earlier times. The Pummerin, since 1957 in the incomplete North or Eagle Tower (60m high), is one of the largest bells in the world. It was cast in 1711 from the metal of captured Turkish cannons and originally hung in the South Tower. It plummeted down in the fire of April 1945 and broke into smithereens. It was cast again from the pieces, and now annually peals in the New Year, and is to be heard all over Vienna.

Reticulated vaulting up to 27 meters

*The "Fenstergucker" – self-portrait of*
*A. Pilgram on the pulpit (1514)*

*Saint Stephen's Cathedral*

5

*Organ foot (Master Pilgram)*

high and supported by 18 columns spans the interior of the cathedral and its three aisles. The high altar from Johann Jakob Pock (1640-1647) is worked in black marble and carries a depiction painted on pewter plates of the stoning of St Stephanus (the first Christian martyr). Far more important, however, is the "Wiener Neustadt Altar" in the side nave to the left, a Gothic winged altar from 1447. In the middle shrine is depicted the Coronation of the Virgin, as well as St Barbara (with the tower), and St Katharina (with the wheel). The

*Gothic pulpit*

inner wings show the Life of Mary and Jesus. On the altar are the differingly interpreted vowels "AEIOU"–the initials of Friedrich III's motto (Austria erit in orbe ultima – Austria will exist until the end of the world; or Austriae est imper- are orbi universo – the whole world is at the service of Austria). Friedrich III's sar- cophagus, design by Niclas Gerhaert van Leyden, and cut from red marble, stands at the front in the side aisle to the right. The gravestone slab shows the emperor in coronation robes; the side reliefs from Max Valmet and Michael

*Miraculous picture of Maria Pócs*

*Servant Madonna*

Tischer deal with the imperial foundations. With four manuals, 125 registers and around 10,000 pipes, the "giant organ" is one of the largest in Europe. On it oldest part, the Late Gothic organ foot (1513), its creator, Anton Pilgram, is immortalised as a bust. A further self-portrait of Pilgram, seen peering through a window ("Fenstergucker"), is found on the Gothic pulpit he made in sandstone between 1514 and 1515. On its steps are depicted toads and lizards as symbols of evil, which are hindered from gaining access by a dog, the symbol of good. Worked in relief in the balustrades are the four church fathers, Ambrosius, Hieronymus, Pope Gregor and Augustinus. The folklore "Servant Madonna" (1320), near the main portal, is also a work of this master of the Early Gothic. A further witness to Gothic building art is the "Capistran Pulpit" (around 1430) from Johannes Capestrano of the Franciscans who called for a crusade against the Turks in 1451. Also worth mentioning are: the miraculous picture of Maria Pócs (1676), a Carpartho-Russian work; the baptismal font from Ulrich Auer in the Chapel of St Catherine, and the Baroque Johann Nepomuk altar (1723) with a painting from Johann Martin Schmidt ("Kremser Schmidt").

*Interior aspect of St Stephen's*

*Capistran Pulpit*

*West choir gallery with the "Giant Organ"*

*Friedrich III's sepulchre*

*Albertinian chancel from the south*

11

## THE HAAS HOUSE

The Haas House was designed by the architect Hans Hollein and completed in 1990.

St Stephen's Cathedral reflects wonderfully in the glass facades of this modern shopping palace.

**THE GRABEN** with the
**STATUE OF THE HOLY TRINITY**
(PEST STATUE)
The former 12th century market square took its name from a moat (Graben) of a Roman castle that was filled in during expansion of the city. In 1679 Emperor Leopold I fulfilled a vow made during the pest epidemic to erected what was first a wooden statue in the Graben in honour the Holy Trinity, which was replaced in 1693 by an imposing marble column (design by M. Rauchmiller).

## THE CHURCH OF ST PETER

Immediately adjacent to the Graben and rising on the walls of an ancient church, this Baroque church, with the richest art treasures in Vienna, was consecrated in 1733. Almost all of the great masters of the day contributed to its decoration, such as M. Rottmayr with his cupola frescoes and M. Altomonte with his altarpieces. Beneath the Altar of the Holy Family are kept the relics of St Donatus.

## THE DONNER FOUNTAIN

Georg Raphael Donner created this fountain ensemble in 1739, the central figure of which personifies Foresight (Lat: Providentia).

*Empress Elisabeth*     *Emperor Franz Joseph*     *Crown-prince Rudolph*

## THE IMPERIAL CRYPT

Beneath the chaste Capuchin Church with its bare facade, which was restored in 1936 according to old plans, lies the last resting place of the members of the Hapsburg dynasty. The only non-Hapsburg laid here is Countess Fuchs, the governess and mentor of Maria Theresa. The imperial couple, Matthias and Anna, began the building in 1618 and placed it in the care of the Capuchin Order. The Imperial Crypt was completed in 1632, long after the death of the founders. It is divided by the sarcophagi of the founders – as well as those of Leopold, Karl, Maria Theresa, Franz, and Ferdinand, and also includes the Tuscany Crypt, the New Crypt, the Franz Joseph Crypt, and the Crypt Chapel.

*Double sarcophagus of Emperor Franz I Stephan von Lothringen and Maria Theresa*

## THE STATE OPERA

The first building on the Ringstrasse (Vienna's elegant inner-ring road), the Court Opera Theatre, was completed in 1869. The entire planner, August von Siccardsburg, and the interior decorator, Eduard van der Nüll, who both construc-ted this building in accord with the French Renaissance, were subject to extremely sharp criticism. The derision of the people drove van der Nüll to suicide, Siccardsburg had a heart attack shortly after. Both men did not live to see

*State Opera, interior aspect*

*State Opera, Staircase*

the opening of the Court Opera on May 15, 1869, with Mozart's Don Giovanni. The building burned down completely after a bomb attack on March 12, 1945. Rebuilding according the plans of Erich Boltenstern, Ceno Kosak, Otto Possinger and R. H. Eisenmenger, who orientated exactly on historic models, took ten years to complete. The official opening took place on November 5, 1955, with a performance of Beethoven's Fidelio under Karl Böhm.

Great composers and directors such as Gustav Mahler, Richard Strauss, Franz Schalk and Clemens Krauss, were given responsibility for the direction of the State Opera, but the criticism of the "1.6 million co-directors" – as Herbert von Karajan called the Viennese – still gave rise to some despair. The Viennese simply love their opera, and perhaps that is why the house on the Ring is difficult terrain for some opera directors, and still one of the leading opera houses in the world today. A permanent ensemble, with many international stars and the magnificent State Opera Orchestra, make possible the high standard of performances possible. The opera becomes a focal point of social life each year when it opens its doors for the Opera Ball in February.

Rembrandt, "Titus",
Museum of Fine Art

Museum of Fine Art

*Museum of Fine Art, Stairs*

# THE NATURAL HISTORY MUSEUM AND THE MUSEUM OF FINE ART

These two museums flanking the Maria Theresa Square were built in the years between 1872 and 1881. Gottfried Semper dedicated himself principally to the outer form, Karl von Hasenauer assumed responsibility for the interior design. In the vestibule of the Natural History Museum, the ceiling painting by Hans Canon depicts in an impressive way the Circle of Life. The eight departments of the building mediate a unique picture of the biogenesis of flora and fauna. Together with prehistoric and anthropological displays, and the world-famous meteorite collection in the department of minerals, are also displays of the utensils and art objects of our forefathers (e.g. the well-known Venus von Willendorf, a fertility idol

*P. Breughel the Elder, "Farmer's Wedding"*

from the 15th millennium BC). The Museum of Fine Art accommodates one of the most important galleries of painting in the world, and a fabulously rich collection of sculpture and applied arts. Famous, above all, is Benvenuto Cellini's Salzfass (Salt Barrel) from the middle of the 16th century; there is also a coin cabinet, an Egyptian collection with numerous mummies and a collection from the antique world with Greek, Etruscan, Roman, and old Christian works of art. Description of only a small part of the overwhelming number of paintings – a tour runs over almost four kilometres – would be beyond the bounds of this little book, thus, here follows only a brief enumeration of some of the masters represented in this museum: Titian, Tintoretto, Veronese, Caravaggio, Bellotto, Raphael, Velásquez, Rubens, Bosch, Rembrandt, Cranach, van Dyck, Holbein, Dürer and Pieter Breughel. The Museum of Fine Art owns the largest concise collection of paintings of the last named Flemish master.

*Raphael, "Madonna in rural setting"*

## THE PARLIAMENT
This sumptuous building was built between 1873 and 1883 in the style of the Helenic antique period according to designs by Theophil Hansen. The main tract, with eight Corinthian columns, is reminiscent of a Greek temple. The State government of the Austro-Hungarian Empire met here until 1918. The Parliament today is the seat of the National Assembly and the Ministry of State.

## THE PALLAS ATHENE FOUNTAIN
In this fountain ensemble (design: T. Hansen) before the main front of the Parliament is the impressive statue of the Pallas Athena, a work by Karl Kundmann. The Goddess of Wisdom is flanked by the allegorical figures of the legislation and administration (works by J. Tautenhayn), the figures of the gods at the feet of Athena symbolise the rivers Danube and Inn, Elbe and Vltava.

## THE CITY HALL

The sumptuous, palace-like City Hall, which was constructed in the New Gothic style by the cathedral master-builder, Friedrich Schmidt, is somewhat removed from the Ring by the City Hall Park. On the peak of the 98-metre-high middle spire stands the 3.4-meter-high Rathausmann (the City Hall Man). Regular "Arcade Courtyard Concerts" are held here in these imposing surroundings in summer. The City Hall, the office of the mayor and municipal council, can also be seen on tours of the building.

## THE VOTIVE CHURCH

An attempt on the life of Emperor Franz Joseph by an anarchist failed in 1853. In gratitude for his deliverance he built the neo-Gothic Votive Church of "Christ the Saviour" (1856-1879). Heinrich Ferstel produced the plans. In the Baptism Chapel is the sepulchre of Niklas Count Salm (died around 1533) who defended Vienna against the Turks in 1529. The "Antwerp Altar" (to the right of the high altar) is a 15th century work of Flemish carving.

## THE UNIVERSITY

This building, planned and constructed in the Italian Renaissance style by Heinrich Ferstel between 1873 and 1883, is the main building today of what is now the oldest German language university, and was founded by Duke Rudolf IV in 1365. The middle projection of the main facade is a copy of a two-floored Renaissance loggia; a dome-like mansard roof arches above. In the lovely arcade courtyard, the monuments of numerous famous professors are reminders of the great tradition of the Alma Mater Rudolphina.

## THE BURG THEATRE
When the theatre on St Michael's Square, which Joseph II made into the German National Theatre in 1776, had to make way for expansion of the Hofburg during the Ringstrasse era, the new Imperial Court Theatre, the "Burg", was built to replace it. Gottfried Semper (exterior design) and Carl Hasenauer (interior decoration) took their inspiration from the Italian High Renaissance. On the attic of the central building is the 18-metre-long "Bacchanalian Procession", a bas-relief from Rudolf Weyr. Carl Kundmann created the group "Apollo with the Muses Melpomene and Thalia" for the balustrade above. The ceiling paintings over the sumptuous stairway of the side-wing are from Gustav and Ernst Klimt, Franz Matsch, and others. The Burg Theatre remains one of the leading German-language stages to this day.

*Burg Theatre, Stairway*

## THE EMPRESS ELISABETH MEMORIAL

The memorial to the wife of Emperor Franz Joseph I, who was murdered in 1898 in Geneva, was made by Hans Bitterlich in marble. (Architecture by F. Ohlmann.) It was unveiled in the Volksgarten (Folks' Garden) in 1907. Elisabeth of Bavaria was born in Munich in 1837 and the monarch in 1854.

## THE THESEUS TEMPLE

The Theseus Temple in the Volksgarten is a copy of the Theseion in Athens, and was created and completed by Peter Nobile in 1823. Originally stood in it the group "Theseus Conquers the Minotaur" from Antonio Canova (now in the Museum of Fine Art). It occasionally served in our century as a place for archaeological (Ephesus finds) and art exhibitions.

The bronze figure "The Victor" is a work by Josef Müllner (1921).

## THE HELDENPLATZ
(Heroes Square)

This square before the Hofburg takes its name from two great heroes in military history: Archduke Karl, who beat Napoleon I at Aspern, and Prince Eugen of Savoy, the field-marshal so loved in Austria. Anton Fernkorn created the two memorials to the heroes in the middle of the 19th

*Archduke Karl Memorial*

*Prince Eugen Memorial*

century. Because Austria felt threatened by the Turks after their successful war against Venice, Prince Eugen (1663-1736) led his troops into battle on the side of Venice. He conquered the Banat Plain and overran Belgrade, beat the Turkish army, thus taking the fortress.

(The folk-song, Prince Eugen the Noble Knight, is a reminder of his victory.) Austria achieved its greatest territorial expansion through the Passarowitz Treaty (1718).

## THE HOFBURG

The pompous dimensions of this palace are a witness to Austria's power and riches in times past. As a symbol for over 600 years rule of the Hapsburgs, their residence reflects the history of building from the Gothic to the historicism of the Ringstrasse style. Nevertheless, the various styles of the building complex harmonise extremely well. The architects, Gottfried Semper and Karl von Hasenbauer, originally planned to place an identical building opposite the New Hofburg. Thus, together with the museums and the Messepalast (Trade-fair Centre) on the other side of the Ringstrasse, a gigantic "Imperial Forum" was to come into being. This intention was, however, incompletely realised.

The Hofburg today accommodates the offices of the Austrian President (in the Leopold tract), the Ethnological Museum, parts of the Museum of Fine Art, with a collection of old weapons and music instruments, the Ephesus Museum, the Treasure Chamber, the Austrian National Library, the Spanish Riding School – it also contains prestigious premises for international conferences. The various museums and the National Library are housed in the New Burg, which was commissioned by Franz Joseph I, and built by Semper and Hasenauer between 1881 and 1913. The building of the St Michael tract was already begun in 1735 after plans by Joseph Emanuel Fischer von Erlach, but was only completed in 1893. The wrestling and falling Herculean figures flanking the St Michael Portal, and the wall fountains on the facade are special eye-catchers. The wall-fountain sculptures show the allegories "Rulers of the Land" (Edmund Hellmer) and the

*St Michael Tract (portal)*

"Rulers of the Sea" (Rudolf Weyr). Emperor Franz Joseph I's work rooms are in the Imperial Chancellery tract, which was built from 1723 to 1730 by Lukas von Hildebrandt and Fischer von Erlach between the St Michael Square and the Ballhaus (Ball House) Square of today. Franz Joseph's wife, the Empress Elisabeth, had her apartment in the Baroque Amalienburg.

*The "Most High Court Table"*

## THE SWISS COURT

The oldest preserved tract in the Hofburg was begun in 1275 by King Ottokar II of the Bohemian House of
Przemysl. Rudolf I von Hapsburg con-
tinued the building. During expansion in
the Renaissance Period, the Swiss Portal was built (1536-1553) upon commis-
sion of Emperor Ferdinand I. The name
of the court is taken from the Imperial
Bodyguard, then comprising Swiss sol-
diers in the time of Maria Theresa,
which were housed there. The Swiss
tract today houses the Treasure Chamber with its priceless valuables and real
works of wonder of the finest gold-
smith and jewellers' art.

*Swiss Portal*

*Imperial Apple, Austrian Imperial Crown, Sceptre*

## THE TREASURE CHAMBER

The collection, which is hardly surpassed, dates back to the inheritance of Emperor Maximilian I, and was enriched over the course of time with many art objects from the possessions of the Hapsburgs. It comprises spiritual and secular departments. The central pieces are the crown-treasure of the "Holy Roman Empire of the German Nations" and the crown of Rudolf II (the Imperial Crown of Austria since 1804). Also exhibited are the jewels of Maria Theresa, Archduchess of Austria and Queen of Hungary, the robes of the Knights Order of the Golden Fleece, the insignia of the Austrian archdukes, the Burgundy treasure from the inheritance of Emperor Maximilian I, and many other gems.

## EMPEROR FRANZ JOSEPH I AND EMPRESS ELISABETH

The two life-size portraits from Winter-halter are in the Hofburg today where the imperial couple had their chambers. Franz Joseph I (1830-1916), as Emperor of Austria and King of Hungary, steered the destiny of the double monarchy. With his assumption of office in the government in 1848, the development of Vienna enjoyed tremendous revival. The old fortifications were demolished; the representative Ringstrasse replaced them with monumental palaces and gardens. The creation of cultural, social – and not least – sanitary facilities, showed the Emperor's humanitarian spirit. His wife Empress Elisabeth, so lovingly called "Sissi" by the people, from the House of Wittelsbach, fell victim to assassination in Geneva in 1898.

## THE AUSTRIAN NATIONAL LIBRARY

The former Court Library on Josef's Square was built according to the plans of Johann Bernhard Fischer von Erlach by his son Joseph Emanuel between 1723 and 1735. The sumptuous hall is among the magnificent room creations of the Late Baroque. Daniel Gran created the splendid frescoes: in the cupola are the allegories of various sciences; on the ceiling is a depiction of Emperor Karl VI, who commissioned the building. Peter and Paul von Strudel, placed him in the middle of the cupola room as a marble statue, which is surrounded by sixteen other statues of the Habsburgs.

The priceless collections of the National Library comprise over 2.2 million hand-written and printed manuscripts,

among which are the valuable leather-bound volumes from the inheritance of Prince Eugen, as well as numerous maps, musical notations and historical material of the theatre.

## THE SPANISH RIDING SCHOOL

Joseph Fischer von Erlach completed the "Winter Riding School" (between the Swiss Court and the Court Stables) in 1735. The sumptuous baroque Great Hall, with its gallery supported by sixteen Corinthian columns, formed the magnificent framework for numerous festive events at the time of the Vienna Congress. The classical art of riding, throughout the world only cultivated in Vienna today, now takes place there. Riders wear historical uniforms during performances. It is the oldest riding school in the world, and originated from the "Spanish Riding Stables", which were known as early as 1572.

The Lipizzaner, black as foals, later with rare exceptions, white, are a crossbreed of Andalusian, Arab, and Neapolitan horses. They once proved themselves not only in battle, but were also used in the popular horse ballets and they drew the carriage of Emperor Franz Joseph. These unique horses are bred today at the national stud at Piber near Köflach in Styria.

## THE CHURCH OF ST MICHAEL

Looking from the cupola room of the St Michael tract of the Hofburg to the church opposite, one sees dazzling wrought-iron work in the St Michael Portal. St Michael Square before it is surrounded by important buildings: the Hofburg, the Loos House and the Church of St Michael, the former court parish church of the Imperial House of Austria. They are, in part, from the 13th century, but were often rebuilt and extended in the course of history. The slender spire is still of the Gothic period, the portal front-structure is a work by Antonio Beduzzi of the Baroque period. Ferdinand von Hohenberg designed the classic facade in 1792. The "Fall of the Angel" theme accompanies us through the church to a sandstone group from Lorenzo Mattielli on the portal front structure, further on as a colossal painting from Michelangelo Unterberger above the right transept arm, as well as the richly detailed stucco work from Karl Georg Merville on the eastern end of the chancel. The interior of the three-aisled church is rich in art treasures. In the tower chapel, next to the entrance, are fresco remains of the 13th century depicting St Cosma, St Thomas and St Damian, as well as the 14th century "Mass of St Gregor". The picture of the "Fourteen Helpers in Need" on the Johann Nepomuk Altar (1643) is from T. Pock. On the altar of the sumptuous Vespers Chapel is a pietà in wood (circa 1430). The church is also famous for

the grave memorials of important aristocrats.

## "LOOS HOUSE" ON THE ST MICHAEL SQUARE

The Art Nouveau architect, Adolf Loos, built this residential and commercial house in 1910 for the men's fashion firm of Goldman and Salatsch. The facade design seemed so revolutionary and bold to the Viennese that building had to be temporarily stopped.

Even Emperor Franz Joseph disliked the unframed "windows without eye-brows". Loos separated clearly the smoothly clad residential part from the business premises with Cipollino marble on the exterior, and with his ideas he was a forerunner in building in a new and functional way. The "Kärntner Bar" (Kärntner Passage, in the 1st District) from the year 1907, is an example of his genius for interior design.

## THE FRANZ JOSEPH MEMORIAL

The statue showing the emperor in military uniform was brought only in 1957 from Wiener Neustadt to the Burg Garden in Vienna.

## THE MOZART MEMORIAL

Viktor Tilgner created this statue in 1896 in honour of the great composer, Wolfgang Amadeus Mozart. Born in Salzburg in 1756, Mozart came to Vienna in 1781, where many of his greatest works were performed. He was buried in 1791 in the St Marx Graveyard in Vienna.

## THE BUTTERFLY HOUSE
In this, one of the world's loveliest Art Nouveau houses, you will feel the magic of a tropical rain forest with hundreds of exotic butterflies. Independent of external temperatures, rain or snow, you will submerge yourself in a fantastic world of animals, plants, giant trees and waterfalls.

## THE COURT CHURCH (old Jesuit church)

The Jesuits, who were called to Vienna in 1551 in the cause of the Counter Reformation, renovated the old Court Carmelite Church between 1607 and 1610 in the Baroque style. Carlo Antonio Carlone gave the facades their present form in 1662. With the disbanding of the Jesuit Order, the Church of the Virgin "Of the Nine Choirs of Angels" became a city parish church. Pope Pius VI personally hurried to Vienna in 1782 to alleviate Joseph II's anticlerical reforms, and bestowed the Easter blessing from the church balcony.

## THE CITIZENS' ARSENAL

Originally erected as an arsenal for the citizens of Vienna, it serves today as a fire-station headquarters. The figurative decoration of the Baroque facades is from Lorenzo Mattielli.

## THE MARRIAGE FOUNTAIN
(JOSEF'S FOUNTAIN)

Leopold I vowed in 1702 to erect a column to St Josef if his son, Joseph I, took the fortifications at Landau and returned safely. Under Karl VI, the original wooden column was replaced by a marble fountain from J. E. Fischer von Erlach (1732) that shows the marriage of Mary and Joseph.

## MARIA AM GESTADE

A Gothic building gem rises on Roman foundations over the former branch of the Danube (the "Salzgries" today). Prayer houses for boatsmen were said to have stood here since the 9th century. The church was first mentioned in documents in 1158. The chancel and tower are from the 14th century. The nave and the open filigree spire was completed in 1414 by Michael Knab.

The Gothic glass windows from the 14th century are famous. The sarcophagus and altar of the Holy Redemptorist, Clemens Maria Hofbauer, is a memorial to the patron saint of Vienna.

# THE ANCHOR CLOCK

The bridge-like connection between the houses numbered 10 and 11 on the Hohe Markt bears an artistic clock after the plans of the painter Franz von Matsch (1913). Daily at twelve noon, its mechanism has twelve figures, or pairs of figures – depictions of eminent personalities from the history of Vienna – parading past the old city coat of arms. The figures include Marcus Aurelius, Charles the Great, Duke Leopold VI, Walter von der Vogelweide, Rudolf I, Prince Eugen, Maria Theresa, and Joseph Haydn.

# THE GREEK TAVERN

"Zum Roten Dachl" (Griechengasse)
Even the "liebe Augustin" (a Viennese character) is said to have often dropped in at this medieval tavern during the time of the great pest. The tavern received its name in the 18th century when many trades people from Greece and the Levant lived here. Prominent artists and politicians (Wagner, Strauß, Grillparzer, Nestroy, Lueger, Brahms and Waldmüller) spent time here, not least for to the excellent beer.

## THE CHURCH OF ST RUPRECHT

This venerable little church is considered the oldest sacred building in Vienna. It was founded in 740, the significant parts of the building are from the 11th century. The glass paintings in the middle chancel window (13th century) are among the oldest in Vienna. Around 20 windows were redesigned in the years 1953, 1992 and 1993 by Lydia Roppolt.

## THE SPA SALON IN THE CITY PARK

The Spa Salon was opened in 1867, and has since been a place where the light-hearted muse of the waltz and operetta era has been cultivated. Eduard Strauß once made music here, as well as the magnificent imperial military bands in their famous "promenade concerts".

## THE JOHANN STRAUSS MEMORIAL

(in the City Park)
A private committee, and the Vienna City Council, made the money available for the bronze statue of the composer and the marble relief created by E. Hellmer and unveiled it in 1921.
Johann Strauß (son) was born in Vienna in 1825 and died in 1899 after an eventful and glorious life in the service of the waltz and operetta in the city of his birth.

*The Great Hall of the "Vienna Music Society"*

## THE MUSIC SOCIETY BULDING

The Great or "Golden" Hall, known in short as the "Music Society", was built by Theophil Hansen between 1867 and 1869 for the "Society of the Friends of Music". It is beyond doubt the focal point of Vienna's musical life. It is, so to speak, the home of the Vienna Philharmonic, and their New Years Concert is transmitted by television from here to many countries. Musicians from all over the world have been guests here under the golden caryatids and they praise, like the listeners, the incomparable acoustics.

## THE CHARLES CHURCH

The pest again raged in Vienna in 1713 and KARL VI made a vow to build a church in honour of St Karl Borromäus when it ended. This, Vienna's most significant Baroque sacred building was begun by Johann Bernard Fischer von Erlach in 1716, and completed by his son Joseph Emanuel in 1739. Johann Christoph Mader created the two 33-metre-high Triumph Columns after the Trajan Columns in Rome, whose spiral reliefs relate from the life of St Charles. Columns, facade elements and the 72-metre-high cupola harmonise exquisitely together.

*Detail of the cupola with frescoes from Johann M. Rottmayr*

*High Altar from Johann Bernard Fischer von Erlach*

## THE SCHWARZENBERG PALACE

The uncompleted building by J. Lukas von Hildebrandt was purchased by Adam Prince of Schwarzenberg in 1716. Johann Bernard, and later his son Joseph Emmanuel Fischer von Erlach, completed it in 1728. Daniel Gran's valuable frescoes were largely destroyed during the Second World War.

## THE HIGH-JET FOUNTAIN

Anton Gabrielli financed the fountain from his payment as the builder of the first high-spring water conduit in Vienna (1873). It was redesigned as an illuminated fountain in 1906. The numbers and grouping of the individual jets relate to the number of the weeks, months and days in the year; 12 high jets symbolise the months, 24 lower jets, the hours. On the occasion of the liberation of Vienna by the Red Army, the Liberation Memorial was built behind the high-jet fountain in 1945. The Russian military were responsible for the plans and building. It shows the figure of a Red Guard (12m) on a 20-metre-high column before a balustrade.

# BELVEDERE PALACE

Prince Eugen of Savoy, victor over the Turks and the "secret" emperor, had this Baroque summer residence built by Johann Lukas von Hildebrandt. It comprises two palaces and the magnificent garden laid out by the Bavarian, Dominique Girard. The major part of the complex was completed in 1725. The Upper Belvedere served for prestige, the prince resided in the Lower Belvedere in summer. After his death, his inheritor sold the property to the Hapsburgs. Joseph II accommodated the collection of imperial paintings here in 1777. In 1806 was added the collection from Ambras Palace in Tyrol, which had become a part of Bavaria under Napoleon. In 1890 the two collections were brought to the newly built Museum of Fine Art on the Ringstrasse. Franz Ferdinand, the heir to the throne who was later murdered in Sarajevo, resided in the Upper Belvedere temporarily from 1894. The composer Anton Bruckner lived until his death in 1896 in the custodian tract. The Austrian State International Treaty was signed in the great marble hall of the Upper Belvedere on May 15, 1955, which ended the

occupation of the victorious powers of the Second World War. Austria was again free.

The entire Belvedere today is available to the Austrian Gallery. The Lower Belvedere houses the Austrian Baroque Museum, with sculpture art and paintings from the 17th and 18th centuries. In the Lower Belvedere Orangery is a museum of medieval Austrian art showing works of art from the 12th to the 16th centuries. The gallery of the 19th and 20th centuries in the Upper Belvedere comprises departments for Classicism, Biedermeier, the Ringstrasse Era, Art Nouveau and the largest collection of the works of Klimt, Schiele and Kokoschka.

*Lower Belvedere*

*Mirror Hall. Lower Belvedere, "Apotheosis of Prince Eugen" (marble, B. Permoser)*

*Great Marble Hall*

*Gustav Klimt: "The Kiss"*

## THE ART NOUVEAU HOUSES

Otto Wagner, the great city planner in Vienna at the turn of the century, constructed two residential buildings in the Linke Wienzeile, partly at his own cost, to foster expression for his polychromatic facade design. The house number 38 received its facade decoration from Kolo Moser. Striking plant ornamentation impresses on the front of number 40, the "Majolica House".

## THE SECESSION

Engaged artists in Vienna in 1897 undertook the separation from the "isms" academic traditions with the founding of the "Vienna Secession". Between 1897 and 1898, Josef M. Olbrich, a pupil of Otto Wagner, built the exhibition building – known in short as the "Secession" – for the movement to which belonged Josef Hoffmann, Gustav Klimt and other important Art Nouveau artists. On the cuboid elements of the "Temple of Art" rests the bronze cupola shaped like a laurel bush.

## THE THEATER AN DER WIEN LINKE WIENZEILE

Emanuel Schikaneder, the lyricist of Mozart's Magic Flute, had a theatre constructed between 1798 and 1801 on the Wien (river) that was to become one of the capital's most richly traditional houses. Beethoven wrote his opera Fidelio for the Theater an der Wien. His Violin Concerto was premiered here. From 1831, Johann Nestroy celebrated his triumphant successes. Later, in the Golden (Strauß, Millöcker, Zeller) and Silver (Lehár, Eysler, Kálmán) Eras of the Operetta, the programmes were dedicated to the "light-hearted" muse.

## THE FLEA MARKET
Wienzeile

Every Saturday the Vienna Flea Market takes place in the area at the end of the "Naschmarkt" (food market). It offers lovers of junk valuable objects of yesteryear, and the year before that, mixed with kitsch and the worthless. One should start out early to find a piece of any beauty.

## SCHÖNBRUNN PALACE

Around 1619, Emperor Matthias discovered the "beautiful fountain" – which was said to have given the later sumptuous building its name – when hunting in the area of the palace grounds of today. Johann Bernhard Fischer von Erlach was commissioned in 1695 by Leopold I to construct on the site of the "Katterburg", which was destroyed by the Turks, a palace to surpass even Versailles in glory. For financial reasons, however, a simpler version was decided upon. Between 1744 and 1749, under Maria Theresa, Nicolaus Pacassi extended the building. By 1765 it has received its park design, as seen today, according to French patterns. With its clipped walls of trees, avenues, carpets of flowers, lawns and fountains, it counts among the loveliest in Europe. The Zoo was already laid out by 1752. The Roman Ruin came into being later in 1778, the "Beautiful Fountain" pavilion in 1779, the "Neptune Fountain" in 1780 at the foot of the rise on which Ferdinand von Hohenberg constructed the

"Gloriette" in 1775, and the Palm House in 1883. The Palace Theatre from 1749 received in 1767 its sumptuous Rococo furnishing and served Haydn and Mozart as performance venues. One of the greatest collections of historical luxury and utility carriages is in the Wagenburg, the former Winter Riding School. The most splendid piece in the exhibition is without doubt the Imperial Carriage, the State Carriage of the Vienna Court. After the Hofburg, Schönbrunn has been the preferred residence since the time of Maria Theresa. History has taken place in many of the 1441 rooms and halls. Joseph II married Isabella von Parma here in 1760, and his second wife, Josefa of Bavaria, in 1765. In 1805 and 1806, and again in 1809, the palace was Napoleon's headquarters, and in 1814 and 1815 the Vienna Congress danced in its halls. Emperor Franz Joseph was born in Schönbrunn in 1830, and he died there in 1916. The last emperor, Karl I, renounced the crown here in 1918, thus ending the monarchy in Austria.

# MARIA THERESA

Archduchess of Austria
The oldest daughter of Emperor Karl VI was born in Vienna in 1717. Just on 19, she married for love Franz Stefan von Lothringen in 1736, and give birth to 16 children. When her husband was crowned German emperor in 1745, Maria Theresa refused to be crowned with him – apparently out of parsimony. The "Empress" – who was not an empress at all – made numerous innovations, including the introduction of general compulsory schooling, or the abolition of serfdom. She died in Vienna in 1780 and was buried in the Emperor's Crypt.

*Gloriette*

*Palm House*

*"Tapestry Salon"*

*"Vieux Laque Room"*

"Round Chinese Room"

"Marie Antoinette Room"

60

*Great Gallery*

"Beautiful Fountain"

Lion in the Zoo

Wagenburg, "Imperial Carriage"

## THE ART HOUSE

Since 1991, the Vienna Art House has been located a few minutes' walk from the Hundertwasser House. Its artistic design was directed by Friedensreich Hundertwasser. The works of the master and other artists are shown here in changing exhibitions.

## THE HUNDERTWASSER HOUSE
Friedensreich Hundertwasser, the important Viennese painter and academy professor with a great dislike of geometric lines, realised a vision of new, ecologically related living with this Vienna Council residential building (completed in 1985).

## THE PRATER

After Joseph II made the former imperial hunting grounds in the Prater water-meadows open to the public in 1766, the area developed into a popular and convenient place of recuperation for the Viennese. Coffee houses, stands and places to eat opened, and the "Wurstelprater" (Folk's Prater) soon came into being with its many possibilities for passing the time, and its amusement for young and old. Basilio Calafati erected in 1840 his famous carousel "The Great Chinese", and the "Wurstel", the Punch figure of the puppet shows, copes with countless hair-raising adventures. The giant Ferris wheel was erected in 1897. After the destruction in the last days of the war, in 1945, the Wurstelprater was rebuilt and modernised: The Lilliput Railway travels between the giant Ferris wheel and the Prater Stadium; there are big-dippers, swings, carousels, shooting galleries, haunted tunnels and two-way mirror cabinets, and those wishing to let of steam punches the "Watschenman".

## THE GIANT VIENNA FERRIS WHEEL

The landmark of the State capital. It was erected between 1896 and 1897 by the English engineer, Walter B. Basset. All of the coaches and operating facilities were destroyed in 1945 during the last days of the war, but a year later the giant Ferris wheel again turned on its half-metre-thick and ten-metre-long axle. The diameter of the

wheel is 61 metres, the highest point is 64.75 metres. The entire construction, with its 120 spikes, weighs 403.05 tons.

The views to be enjoyed over Vienna from the slowly turning wheel is famous.

### THE DANUBE TOWER
This 252-metre observation tower was erected under the direction of Hannes Lintl and Robert Krapfenbauer. One reaches the 165-metre-high observation terrace within a few seconds by lift. Above the terrace is a restaurant and a café which turn slowly and offer majestic views of Vienna.

### THE DANUBE PARK
This park of around one square kilometre was laid out between the Old and the New Danube on the occasion of the Vienna International Garden Show in 1964. It is a popular and convenient place for the Viennese to relax and recuperate. The Danube Tower is the focal point of the park.

### THE DANUBE ISLAND
Despite regulation of the Danube in the 19th century, the river still occasionally carried high water. A relief channel was therefore dug in 1972, thus creating a 20-kilometre-long island, which soon became a popular centre for recreation.

## THE UNO CITY

The United Nations made Vienna its third official seat, with New York and Geneva, in 1979. The Vienna International Centre was built between 1973 and 1979 after plans by Johann Staber. It is a massive construction of glass and concrete, and work is carried out there by UNO employees from over 100 countries. Austria joined the world organisation in 1955 after achieving independence. Vienna has been the headquarters of several international organisations since 1957.

## THE MILLENNIUM TOWER

With a total height of 202 metres, respectively, 50 storeys, the Millennium Tower is Austria's highest building and also counts among the highest office buildings in Europe. Together with office space and apartments, there are over 50 shops, restaurants and cafés in the Millennium City.

## THE SPITTELAU REFUSE-BURNING PLANT

The Spittelau Refuse-Burning Plant is another building which, under the direction of Hundertwasser's re-designing, became a richly colourful addition to the face of Vienna. With the new design of the long-distance energy plant, the master gives proof that industrial building can still be perfectly pleasing to the eye.

## GRINZING

Grinzing became a district of Vienna in 1892, and has clearly maintained its character as a vintner's village among the new-wine localities such as Sievering, Nußdorf, Salmannsdorf and Neustift am Wald. The greater part of the picturesque heart of the community is from

the 16th and 17th centuries. The new wine is made from the grapes of the sur-rounding vineyards, and it has made a philosopher of many a good man.

## THE BEETHOVEN HOUSE

The Beethoven House is in the Probus-gasse not far from the one at the Market Square. He lived in this house in 1802 due to the nearby medicinal springs. 25 years before death, he wrote the "Heiligenstadt Testament" – the shattering manifesto of his experiences in life.

## THE LEOPOLDSBERG
Emperor Leopold I laid the foundation stone in 1679, dedicated to the Babenberg margrave, St Leopold III, which was later destroyed by the Turks. After the victory over the invaders he vowed to restore the little church and gave the rise on which it stood the saint's name. The so-called "Babenberg Castle" was burned down in the first Turkish invasion in 1529, and was never rebuilt.

## THE KAHLENBERG
The Order of the Camaldules founded a hermitage in 1629 on the previously uninhabited rise. It was destroyed in 1683 by the Turks, and rebuild somewhat smaller. It was secularised in 1782. In 1783, however, the abandoned church was again consecrated (St Josef). The Sobieski Chapel is a reminder of the historic mass read in the Chapel of St George (on the Leopoldsberg of today) in 1683 by the papal legate, Marco d'Aviano, to the relief army on the morning before the battle against the Turks. Jan III Sobieski, King of Poland, and a significant participant in the victory of Emperor Leopold I's army, was a server at this mass. A copy of the "Black Madonna" from Tschenstochau indicates the service to the church by Polish priests.

## KAHLENBERG AND LEOPOLDSBERG

These are the rises in the Vienna Woods, and thus the last of the Alps. It was from here that the Christian army moved in a decisive confrontation against the Turks in 1683. On the morning before the battle, a mass was celebrated in which the Polish king, Jan Sobieski, served. The relief army achieved a victory of world-wide historical importance, and the threat of Islam spreading in Europe was hindered.

## KLOSTERNEUBURG

Margrave Leopold III built the Romanesque Monastery Church of Klosterneuburg, and later gave it to the Augustine Canons. The world-famous Verdun Altar (Nikolaus von Verdun, 1181) was originally created as a lectern cover; it was made into a grave altar in 1331 for Leopold III (canonised in 1485). In the 17th and 18th centuries, the best artists worked upon the Baroque refurbishment of the interior. Emperor Karl VI wished to have the monastery extended to a palace cloister in the manner of Escorial (Fischer von Erlach the Younger). Around a quarter of the plans were real-

*Black Madonna*

ised. The cupolas of the symbolic-like complex bear the Romeo-Germanic imperial crown, and the duke's hat as an imposing addition. F. Schmidt extended the church towers in the New Gothic style in the 19th century.

## LIECHTENSTEIN CASTLE

Maria Enzersdorf; destroyed by the Turks; restored in the Romantic style in 1873; centre of a romantic nature reserve with several artificial ruins ("Black Tower","Amphitheatre").

## MÖDLING
## (LOWER AUSTRIA)

Mödling was already mentioned in documents in 907; it was raised to a market town in 1443, and to a town in 1875. It was very popular among the Romantics for its "picturesque" location. The Late Gothic Parish Church of St Othmar was destroyed by the Turks shortly after its completion. It was restored in the Baroque style only after 1700. The charnel house next to the church is of the Romantic period (12th century).

Around 1700, a circular Baroque clock-tower was added. The Romanesque rounded-arch portal, with the knotted columns, fascinates with its simple and clear ornamentation. The cultivated face of the town is supported not least by the many old houses (such as the Renaissance Town Hall, Schrannenplatz; or the Sgraffito House, Rathausgasse 6) giving it the reputation of "romantic" Mödling. The Baroque "Statue of the Holy Trinity" (1714) was donated on the occasion of a renewed outbreak of the pest in 1713.

*Town Hall*

## THE LAKE GROTTO IN THE HINTERBRÜHL (LOWER AUSTRIA) NEAR MÖDLING

(southern city border of Vienna)
In 1912, after an explosion in the gypsum mine of the day, more than 20 million litres of water flowed into its passages and tunnels. Thus was formed the largest subterranean lake in Europe. The mine was closed after the catastrophe, and only discovered by cave explorers in the thirties, and made open to the public.

The "Lake Grotto" was confiscated

during the Second World War. The world's first jets were produced in the protective tunnels.

The "Lake Grotto" was reopened after the war and is today a tourist attraction of the first rank.

*Motorboat ride on the subterranean lake*

*Model of the HE 162 Jet*

## MAYERLING (LOWER AUSTRIA)

The plain Mayerling Baroque Palace was the scene of a not entirely explained tragedy in 1889. On January 30, Crown-prince Rudolf, the son of Emperor Franz Joseph, shot first his lover, Baroness Mary Vetsera, and then committed suicide. The emperor then gave the property to the Carmelites. The crown-prince's rooms were demolished. The alter room of the monastery is in their place today.

## HEILIGENKREUZ (NEAR BADEN)

St Leopold III founded in 1133 this Cistercian monastery at the prompting of his son, Otto von Freising. It's name comes from a particle of the holy cross, which Leopold V gave to the monastery in 1188. The Monastery of the Assumption of the Virgin, with its oldest Romanesque parts, is from the 12th century. The cloister, with its 300 marble columns to the south of the church, was constructed between 1220 and 1250. The original grisaille panes are still preserved in the well-house windows (1295). From 1641 to 1674, and from 1683 to 1691, the new, large monastery church was built following destruction by the Turks. Heiligenkreuz is the resting place of some of the Babenbergs.

## BADEN NEAR VIENNA (LOWER AUSTRIA)

The hot sulpha springs, flowing here from a geological split in the earth, were already known to the Romans. Baden enjoyed a great period of popularity in the 19th century. The imperial family chose the town for decades as a summer residence. After the fire of 1812, rebuilding took place in the spirit of J. Kornhäusel; the aristocracy and wealthy citizens built delightful villas here. Prominent names from the world of art, commerce and politics introduced themselves here and made use of the power of the medicinal waters. The "Imperial Residence of the Biedermeier" has remained a spa town of international rank to this day.

*Column of the Holy Trinity*

# INDEX

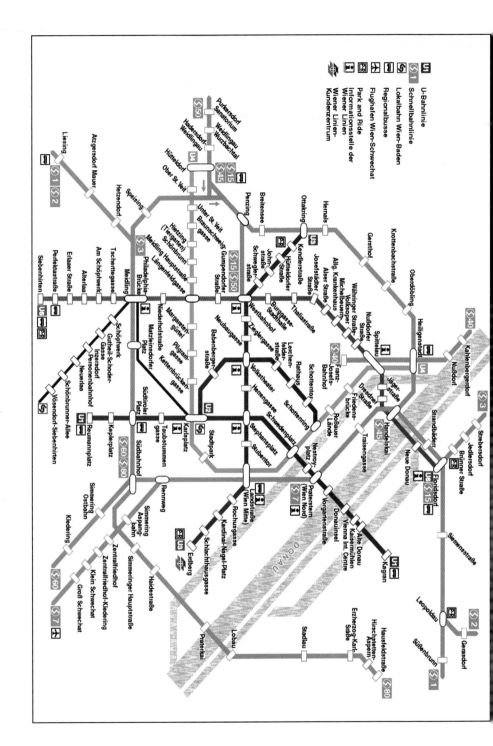

U-Bahnlinie
Schnellbahnlinie
Lokalbahn Wien–Baden
Regionalbusse
Flughafen Wien–Schwechat
Park and Ride
Informationsstelle der Wiener Linien
Wiener Linien-Kundenzentrum